How to Play Funny Fill-In!

Love to create amazing stories? Good, because this one stars YOU. Get ready to laugh with all your friends—you can play with as many people as you want! Make sure to keep this book on your shelf. You'll want to read it again and again!

Are You Ready to Laugh?

- One person picks a story—you can start at the beginning, the middle, or the end of the book.

- Ask a friend to call out a word that the space asks for—noun, verb, or something else—and write it in the blank space. If there's more than one player, ask the next person to say a word. Extra points for creativity!

- When all the spaces are filled in, you have your very own Funny Fill-In. Read it out loud for a laugh.

- Want to play by yourself? Just fold over the page and use the cardboard insert at the back as a writing pad. Fill in the blank parts of speech list, and copy your answers into the story.

Make sure you check out the amazing **Fun Facts** that appear on every page!

Parts of Speech

To play the game, you'll need to know how to form sentences. This list of the parts of speech and the examples will help you get started:

Noun: The name of a person, place, thing, or idea
Examples: tree, mouth, creature
*The **ocean** is full of colorful **fish**.*

Adjective: A word that describes a noun or pronoun
Examples: green, lazy, friendly
*My **silly** dog won't stop laughing!*

Verb: An action word. In the present tense, a verb usually ends in –s or –ing. If the space asks for past tense, changing the vowel or adding a –d or –ed to the end usually will set the sentence in the past.
Examples: swim, hide, play (present tense); biked, rode, jumped (past tense)
*The giraffe **skips** across the savanna.*
*The flower **opened** after the rain.*

Adverb: A word that describes a verb and usually ends in –ly
Examples: quickly, lazily, soundlessly
*Kelley **greedily** ate all the carrots.*

Plural: More than one
Examples: mice, telephones, wrenches
*Why are all the **doors** closing?*

Silly Word or Exclamation: A funny sound, a made-up word, a word you think is totally weird, or a noise someone or something might make
Examples: Ouch! No way! Foozleduzzle! Yikes!
*"**Darn!**" shouted Jim. "These cupcakes are sour!"*

Specific Words: There are many more ways to make your story hilarious. When asked for something like a number, animal, or body part, write in something you think is especially funny.

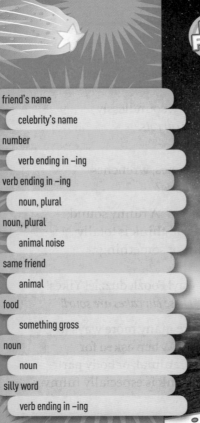

- friend's name
  - celebrity's name
- number
  - verb ending in –ing
- verb ending in –ing
  - noun, plural
- noun, plural
  - animal noise
- same friend
  - animal
- food
  - something gross
- noun
  - noun
- silly word
  - verb ending in –ing

4

Fun Fact! THIRTY-FIVE YEARS AGO A MYSTERIOUS **72-SECOND PULSE** WAS DETECTED THAT CAME FROM A LONG WAY FROM EARTH. **IT'S NEVER BEEN REPEATED.**

INCOMING MESSAGE

A Message From Space

It was the perfect night for stargazing. _____ and I were lying on the roof of _____
(friend's name)   (celebrity's name)

Laboratory, where scientists work as alien hunters. For _____ years, my friend has searched for other
(number)

beings in space. The job involves a lot of _____ and _____ . So tonight, to pass
(verb ending in –ing)   (verb ending in –ing)

the time, we're watching _____ whiz by overhead and tracing _____ in the sky.
(noun, plural)   (noun, plural)

In the background, the lab equipment made a(n) _____ sound as it scanned the universe.
(animal noise)

Just when I asked _____ if the _____ planet was really made of
(same friend)   (animal)

_____ , the sound suddenly got louder. "_____ !" my friend exclaimed.
(food)   (something gross)

This had never happened before, I knew. On the screen of the _____ hooked up to the scanning
(noun)

_____ was a message. It read: "_____ ! We would like to make contact
(noun)   (silly word)

with another life-form in the universe. Is there anyone out there _____ this message?"
(verb ending in –ing)

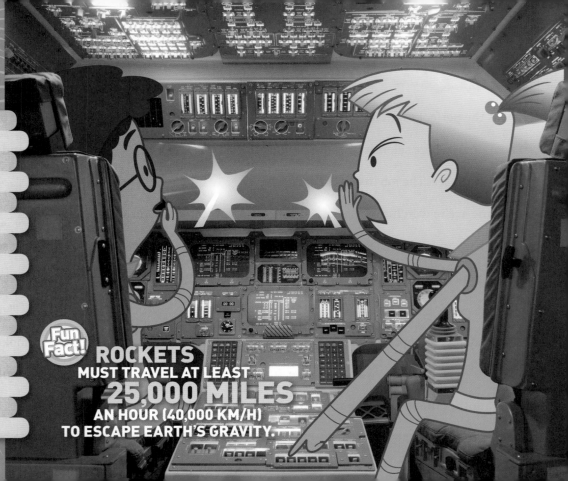

body part, plural

   type of candy bar

friend's name

   color

verb ending in –s

   adverb ending in –ly

noun

   relative's name

adjective

   your hometown

verb

   something enormous

electronic gadget, plural

   direction

famous singer

   noun

Fun Fact! **ROCKETS** MUST TRAVEL AT LEAST **25,000 MILES** AN HOUR (40,000 KM/H) TO ESCAPE EARTH'S GRAVITY.

We can't believe our _____ . An alien message! "We are located in the _____
                     body part, plural   type of candy bar

solar system. Please make contact." Just as _____ and I are about to respond, the screen
                                                      friend's name

turns _____ and the computer _____ ! We decide _____ that we
      color   verb ending in –s   adverb ending in –ly

must go on an expedition to this solar system. First things first: We need a(n) _____ to fly. And
                                                                        noun

we need to learn how to fly. _____ knows where a(n) _____ ship is parked.
                                  relative's name   adjective

We head to _____ , _____ inside the ship, and look at the controls.
                      your hometown   verb

There's a(n) _____ button, so we press it. The _____
                  something enormous   electronic gadget, plural

fire up and blast a hole through the wall. The ship moves _____ . A voice that sounds like
                                               direction

_____ begins speaking—it's the ship's onboard robot. We press another _____
     famous singer   noun

and rocket into space. There's no turning back now.

large number

noun, plural

color

noun

verb ending in –ing

command

noun

silly word

food

noun

verb

friend's name

noun

something sticky

something gross

body part

adjective

noun

body part, plural

Fun Fact!

A SPACE SUIT WEIGHS
280 POUNDS (127 KG)
WITHOUT
AN ASTRONAUT IN IT.

A Wild Spacewalk

We're flying through space at _____ (large number) miles per hour in our ship. It's hard to move, but I

manage a quick look outside and see _____ (noun, plural) . A(n) _____ (color) _____ (noun)

starts _____ (verb ending in –ing) , and the onboard robot warns us: "_____ (command) !" The _____ (noun)

comes to a dead stop. We're stuck in space! I reach into a box labeled "_____ (silly word) " and pull out

a suit made of _____ (food) . I slip it on, open the _____ (noun) and _____ (verb)

outside. _____ (friend's name) holds a(n) _____ (noun) that's attached to me, so I won't drift away.

I see _____ (something sticky) smeared all over the ship. It must be from flying through the cloud of

_____ (something gross) . I use my _____ (body part) to wipe it off, and suddenly I'm stuck

to the ship! Just then, I see a(n) _____ (adjective) _____ (noun) in the distance.

It's headed right for us! I close my _____ (body part, plural) ! "Need help?" a voice says.

friend's name

    temperature

foul odor

    language

adjective ending in –y

    silly word

liquid

    something soft

favorite place

    number

animal

    color

type of bird

    insect, plural

type of drink

    body part, plural

another body part, plural

    size

something gross

Fun Fact!

ASTRONAUTS DRINK RECYCLED URINE.

Dinner With an Alien

_____ and I climb aboard the alien spaceship. It's _____ and smells like _____ .
friend's name   temperature   foul odor

But it's a ride, and we need one—our ship has broken down in space. The alien speaks a little _____ ,
language

so we can communicate somewhat. So far, it seems _____ . After traveling for hours, we land
adjective ending in –y

on the planet _____ . It's raining _____ , and the surface is made of _____ ,
silly word   liquid   something soft

but otherwise it reminds me of _____ . We head to the alien's house for dinner. There's no table;
favorite place

instead we eat off the back of a(n) _____-legged _____ . A(n) _____ _____
number   animal   color   type of bird

serves us something that looks like _____ swimming in _____ .
insect, plural   type of drink

We're disgusted, but the alien is scarfing it up—with its _____ !
body part, plural

We don't want to be rude, so we dig in with our _____ .
another body part, plural

Dessert is even worse, though: It's a(n) _____ bowl of _____ !
size   something gross

silly word

    favorite superhero

type of structure

    color

clothing item, plural

    noun, plural

celebrity's name

    shape

another shape

    time

type of pattern

    instrument

verb

    noun

noun

    body part, plural

animal, plural

    favorite song

noun, plural

Fun Fact! ASTRONAUT ALAN SHEPARD HIT THREE **GOLF BALLS** ON THE MOON WHILE EXPLORING ITS SURFACE IN 1971.

It's day two on planet _____ (silly word), and our alien host wants to take us to watch a game of

_____ (favorite superhero). We enter a(n) _____ (type of structure) and see a crowd of aliens.

This must be a popular sport! The fans are wearing _____ (color) _____ (clothing item, plural) and waving

_____ (noun, plural). They chant "_____ (celebrity's name)!" as the players head onto the field. Half of the

players have _____ (shape) heads; the other half have _____ (another shape) heads. At _____ (time),

an alien with _____ (type of pattern) skin plays a(n) _____ (instrument) and the game begins. From what

we can tell, the object of the game is to _____ (verb) into a(n) _____ (noun) while holding a(n)

_____ (noun). When a team scores, the fans slap their _____ (body part, plural) together. At halftime,

a group of _____ (animal, plural) comes out and dances to _____ (favorite song). The team with the

most _____ (noun, plural) is declared the winner. The crowd goes wild!

friend's name

silly word

number

your hometown

noun

noun

something gross

scary animal, plural

large number

adjective

your age

noun, plural

something enormous

adjective

silly word

number

body part, plural

verb ending in –s

singer

OPEN
MALL
BUY
NOW
SHOP
EAT
STORES
OVER 5000 STORES
OPEN 24 HRS
FREE PARKING

Fun Fact! ASTRONAUT NEIL ARMSTRONG LEFT HIS **SPACE BOOTS** ON THE MOON.

_____ and I have been on planet _____ for _____ weeks now, and we're
(friend's name)   (silly word)   (number)

missing _____ . So we hit the alien mall, in search of _____ and _____ .
        (your hometown)   (noun)   (noun)

The first store sells only _____ , so we leave immediately. We pass a pet store full of
                           (something gross)

_____ . In another store, we try on a few things, but nothing fits—everything
(scary animal, plural)

has _____ armholes. By now we're _____ , so we look for the food court. It's easy to
    (large number)   (adjective)

find because it's where all the _____-year-old aliens hang out. After a quick snack of _____ ,
                                (your age)   (noun, plural)

we get back to shopping. We finally find what we're looking for atop a(n) _____ . Suddenly,
                                                                          (something enormous)

a(n) _____ alien appears and says, "_____ ?" We point to what we want
     (adjective)   (silly word)

and hold up _____ _____ . The alien _____ away and returns with
            (number)   (body part, plural)   (verb ending in –s)

our goods. We pay for them by performing the dance from _____ 's latest video—success!
                                                        (singer)

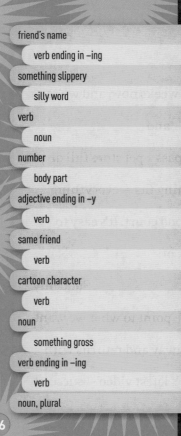

- friend's name
- verb ending in –ing
- something slippery
- silly word
- verb
- noun
- number
- body part
- adjective ending in –y
- verb
- same friend
- verb
- cartoon character
- verb
- noun
- something gross
- verb ending in –ing
- verb
- noun, plural

Fun Fact! SOME ASTRONAUTS LIVING ON THE MIR SPACE STATION **ATE JELL-O EVERY SUNDAY** TO HELP KEEP TRACK OF THE DAYS.

Mind Control

_____ and I are _____ across a field of _____
    friend's name   verb ending in –ing   something slippery

on planet _____ . Our alien friend agreed to _____ us here but refused to
    silly word   verb

get out of the _____ after we landed. We're about _____ miles from the ship when
    noun   number

we meet another alien. It holds out its _____ to shake; we grasp it. But we begin to feel
    body part

_____ . I suddenly have an overwhelming urge to _____ upside-down,
    adjective ending in –y   verb

and _____ starts to _____ backward. Then we start to say, "_____
    same friend   verb   cartoon character

_____ _____ !" over and over. The alien hands us _____ , and we
    verb   noun   something gross

start _____ it into our mouths like it's the best thing we've ever eaten. We've lost control
    verb ending in –ing

of ourselves! I reach out and _____ the alien, to try to break its spell. Just then, a beam of
    verb

_____ hits us. We've been rescued by our alien friend!
    noun, plural

verb ending in –ing

silly word

animal, plural

animal sound

verb

noun, plural

friend's name

same animal, plural

shape

verb ending in –ing

something gross

feeling

adjective

noun

same animal

noun

body part

verb ending in –s

food

Fun Fact! CHIMPANZEES, MONKEYS, DOGS, MICE, AND A GUINEA PIG HAVE ALL **JOURNEYED INTO SPACE.**

I'm on all fours, _____ (verb ending in –ing) like an animal. I'm trying to communicate with the inhabitants

of planet _____ (silly word), which is ruled by _____ (animal, plural). I start to _____ (animal sound),

and the space animals _____ (verb) and stick out their _____ (noun, plural). I keep up the noise, and

_____ (friend's name) and the alien who flew us to this planet join in. The _____ (same animal, plural)

arrange themselves in a _____ (shape) and make a _____ (verb ending in –ing) sound. We start to

copy the sound, and the animals soon offer us a bowl of _____ (something gross). We don't want

to offend them, so we dig in. This makes them _____ (feeling), and they lead us to the

_____ (adjective) _____ (noun) where their leader lives. A _____ (same animal)

emerges, wearing a _____ (noun) on its _____ (body part). It _____ (verb ending in –s)

a few times, says, "_____ (food)," then leaves. We're honored.

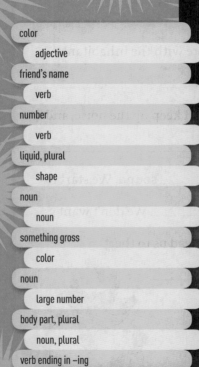

color

    adjective

friend's name

    verb

number

    verb

liquid, plural

    shape

noun

    noun

something gross

    color

noun

    large number

body part, plural

    noun, plural

verb ending in –ing

Fun Fact! A **BLACK HOLE,** WHICH HAS THE STRONGEST **GRAVITATIONAL PULL** IN THE UNIVERSE, CAN FORM FROM A SUPERNOVA— THE EXPLOSIVE **DEATH** OF A VERY LARGE STAR.

A Galactic Close Call

We're flying past a(n) _____ hole, and things are getting _____ . _____
                           color   adjective   friend's name

and I trust our alien pilot, but the holes are known to _____ anything that comes close.
                                                        verb

And we're close—within _____ miles. So we hold tight as the whole ship starts to _____ ,
                             number   verb

and the pilot yells, "Hang on to your _____ !" The lights go out, and we start spinning in a
                                        liquid, plural

_____ . The onboard _____ flies across the ship, colliding with a(n) _____
shape   noun   noun

and spraying _____ everywhere. The lights flicker back on, but flash _____ .
                     something gross   color

The pilot decides we've got to move faster, so it pulls on the overhead _____ and we increase
                                                               noun

our speed to _____ miles per hour. Our _____ press to the back of
               large number   body part, plural

our seats as we soar through a cloud of _____ . We emerge from the other side and
                                               noun, plural

the ship stops _____ . We made it!
               verb ending in –ing

friend's name

planet

noun

verb

noun

verb ending in –ing

verb

language

another planet

noun

noun

adjective

silly word

adverb ending in –ly

room in a house

feeling

same friend

type of dance

large number

Fun Fact!

THE INTERNATIONAL SPACE STATION WEIGHS

861,804 POUNDS

(390,908 KG).

22

A Visit to the Space Station

Our alien friend has had just about enough of _____ and me. We've had
                                                  friend's name

several close calls, so it's dropping us off at the International Space Station, docked above

_____ . The alien presses a(n) _____ in the ship, and we _____
    planet   noun   verb

outside and into a(n) _____ inside the station. Several astronauts _____ aboard it
                          noun   verb ending in –ing

_____ to our side. In _____ , they ask if we're from _____ . We tell them
    verb   language   another planet

all about our _____ explorations and _____ encounters. They think we're _____ .
                  noun   noun   adjective

So we show them a photo of us with an alien on planet _____ . We're _____
                                                          silly word   adverb ending in –ly

taken to the _____ to report to the captain. She's _____ and allows
                room in a house   feeling

_____ and me to stay aboard the station. We quickly settle into zero-gravity life and by the next
  same friend

day have already performed _____ _____ times in midair.
                              type of dance   large number

friend's name

item of clothing, plural

name of friend's pet

something huge

famous athlete

planet

cartoon character

noun

noun, plural

celebrity's name

another planet

something gross

adjective

year

large number

color

silly word

Fun Fact! SCIENTISTS ARE TRACKING **22,000** EARTH-ORBITING PIECES OF **SPACE JUNK.**

Galactic Garbage Collectors

To earn our keep aboard the International Space Station, _____ (friend's name) and I sign up for galactic garbage collection. We report for duty and change into _____ (item of clothing, plural) that smell like _____ (name of friend's pet). We get into our "truck"—a(n) _____ (something huge)-size ship powered by _____ (famous athlete). An autopilot greets us with "Good morning!" before we blast off. Near _____ (planet)'s moon, called _____ (cartoon character), we collect our first piece of space junk: an old _____ (noun) with _____ (noun, plural) sticking out of it. Next, we pick up a floating photo of _____ (celebrity's name) and argue over who gets to keep it. While flying past _____ (another planet), we scoop up a pile of _____ (something gross), and it stinks up the ship. On the _____ (adjective) side of the moon, we retrieve a homework assignment written in _____ (year). We weigh the garbage—_____ (large number) tons!—before firing it into a(n) _____ (color) hole in the nearby _____ (silly word) galaxy. We decide this job definitely doesn't stink.

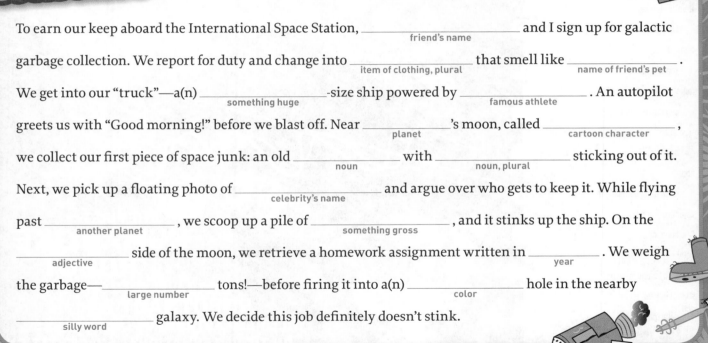

- adjective ending in –est
  - noun, plural
- item of clothing
  - body part, plural
- number
  - friend's name
- noun
  - vegetable, plural
- type of bird
  - animal
- noun
  - something lightweight
- adjective
  - noun, plural
- color
  - verb ending in –ing
- something hot, plural
  - noun, plural
- verb

Fun Fact!

THE FIRST **HUMANLIKE ROBOT** TO TRAVEL INTO SPACE, **ROBOTNAUT 2,** WILL HELP ASTRONAUTS WITH TASKS ON THE INTERNATIONAL SPACE STATION.

Far-Out Gadgets

The International Space Station has all the _____ space gadgets. There are goggles that
adjective ending in –est

let you see _____ that are normally invisible. A special _____ makes
noun, plural   *item of clothing*

your _____ disappear within _____ seconds of putting it on.
body part, plural   *number*

_____'s personal favorite is a(n) _____ that fires _____
friend's name   *noun*   *vegetable, plural*

when you say, "_____ !" One day, while searching for a(n) _____ to fix
type of bird   *animal*

a broken _____ , I find a pair of glasses. I slip them on and look outside. I see clouds of
noun

_____ drift by, _____ _____ spinning through space,
something lightweight   *adjective*   *noun, plural*

bright _____ rays _____ past. Even the sun looks different: Its surface
color   *verb ending in –ing*

is covered in _____ , and a halo of _____ surrounds the star.
something hot, plural   *noun, plural*

These gadgets _____ you a whole new world—make that a whole new universe!
verb

noun

- body part

color

- number

color

- temperature

tropical animal, plural

- body part, plural

liquid

- favorite food

favorite drink

- large number

noun, plural

- something sparkly

pleasant smell

- favorite thing, plural

your name

- favorite celebrity's name

famous singer

Fun Fact!

POPULAR ACTIVITIES

ON THE INTERNATIONAL SPACE STATION INCLUDE RACING, DOING SOMERSAULTS AND BACKFLIPS, AND STARING OUT THE WINDOWS AT SPACE.

A Much-Needed Spacecation

It's paradise here on "New Hawaii." It's a welcome vacation after nearly crashing our _____ several
                                                                                        noun

times, visiting other planets, and escaping one _____ -controlling alien. We're lying on a beach
                                                   body part

under a(n) _____ sky and _____ _____ suns that make the planet a perfect _____ .
            color   number   color   temperature

_____ fan us while robots paint our _____ with _____ .
tropical animal, plural   body part, plural   liquid

For meals, we hit the all-you-can-eat buffet stocked with _____ and _____ .
                                                            favorite food   favorite drink

There are _____ -foot-tall _____ to climb; _____ -filled,
           large number   noun, plural   something sparkly

_____ -scented oceans to swim in; and _____ grow on
pleasant smell   favorite thing, plural

trees. Every evening, after the suns set, fireworks spelling out _____ and
                                                                  your name

_____ light up the sky. Every morning, _____
favorite celebrity's name   famous singer

phones our room for our usual wake-up call. I could stay here forever.

friend's name

    noun

time

    type of candy bar

something round

    fast animal, plural

weird job

    noun, plural

electronic gadget, plural

    adjective

verb

    something small, plural

noun

    large number

something squishy, plural

    favorite song

verb

    body part, plural

IF YOU ARE **12 YEARS OLD** ON EARTH, YOU'D BE ABOUT **6 YEARS OLD ON MARS.**

30

Vacation with _____ is cut short by a message from the International Space Station:
friend's name

"Return to the _____ . At _____ you'll train for a special mission to the
noun _time_

_____ solar system to explore a _____ for possible colonization." We hop onto
type of candy bar _something round_

our space _____ and get back to the ship. There, the _____ gives us our first
fast animal, plural _weird job_

assignment: Learn to use remote _____ . We're given the _____ that control the
noun, plural _electronic gadget, plural_

Mars rovers and two _____ robots that _____ the planet. Our first day in charge, a giant
adjective _verb_

tornado of _____ throws the robots into a deep _____ populated by aliens with
something small, plural _noun_

_____ heads. Using their teeth made of _____ , the aliens try to eat the robots. We hit
large number _something squishy, plural_

the button labeled "_____ ," which starts to blare from the robots. The aliens _____
favorite song _verb_

and cover their _____ . We guide the rovers and the robots back to safety—saved by a song!
body part, plural

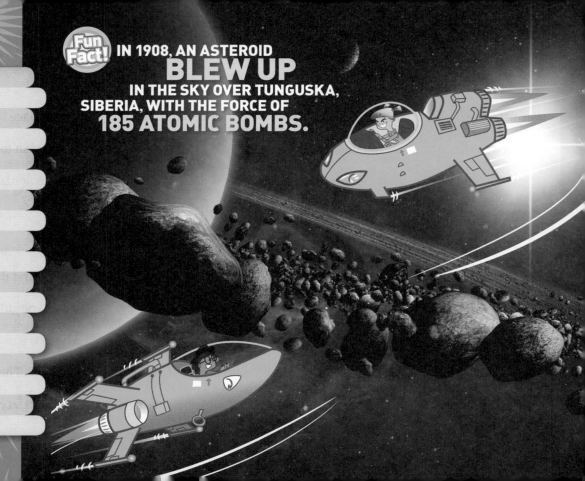

- large number
  - friend's name
- noun, plural
  - silly word
- verb ending in –ing
  - noun
- noun
  - noun, plural
- adjective
  - verb ending in –ing
- another large number
  - body part
- something heavy
  - same friend's name
- food
  - adverb ending in –ly
- noun
  - noun, plural

Fun Fact! IN 1908, AN ASTEROID **BLEW UP** IN THE SKY OVER TUNGUSKA, SIBERIA, WITH THE FORCE OF **185 ATOMIC BOMBS.**

Space Chase

I increase my speed to _____ (large number) miles per hour—the maximum limit. I'm trying to outrun

_____ (friend's name), who's hot on my tail. We're weaving between _____ (noun, plural), deep within the

_____ (silly word) asteroid field. This game of space chase is a lot of fun, but we're actually _____ (verb ending in –ing)

for a mission to another solar system. Today's task: learning to fly a _____ (noun). Just when I think

I've got the hang of things, it collides with a giant _____ (noun). I hit the _____ (noun, plural) and

manage to land on the surface of a(n) _____ (adjective) asteroid, which itself is _____ (verb ending in –ing)

through space at _____ (another large number) miles per hour. I stick my _____ (body part) outside to look

around and just miss being dinged by a passing _____ (something heavy). _____ (same friend's name) pulls

up beside me, yelling, "_____ (food)!" and I _____ (adverb ending in –ly) climb aboard his/her ship. Not before

hitting my ship's self-destruct _____ (noun), though. As we fly away, I watch it explode into _____ (noun, plural).

friend's name

    adjective

color

    noun

noun, plural

    verb

silly word

    noun

body part

    number

noun, plural

    verb

noun

    liquid

noun

    adjective ending in –y

celebrity's name

Fun Fact! TO BIKE TO THE **MOON** YOU WOULD HAVE TO **PEDAL** NONSTOP FOR ABOUT **3** YEARS.

Moon Mission

_____ and I gasp as the moon— _____ and _____ —comes into view. It
     friend's name   adjective   color

looks like a giant _____ suspended in space—beautiful. But landing there isn't so great. The
                        noun

surface is littered with _____ , which causes our ship to _____ and veer
                            noun, plural   verb

off course into a rock. We push the "_____" button to reverse and accidentally roll
                                        silly word

into a(n) _____ . I crane my _____ out the window to inspect the damage
              noun   body part

and notice a set of _____ -toed footprints nearby. We slip into our _____ and
                        number   noun, plural

_____ out of the ship, excited to follow. The tracks lead us across a giant _____
     verb   noun

and around a bubbling pool of _____ . They come to a stop at a(n) _____ .
                                    liquid   noun

There's writing on it: a space message! _____ with excitement, I lean in close and
                                            adjective ending in –y

read aloud the words: "_____ was here!"
                          celebrity's name

planet

food

friend's name

verb ending in –ing

noun, plural

liquid

noun

noun, plural

adjective ending in –er

noun

something sticky

same friend

noun

feeling

same sticky something

noun

noun

same friend

adjective

Fun Fact! IN OUR SOLAR SYSTEM **13 PLANETS** ORBIT OUR STAR, THE SUN. SCIENTISTS HAVE IDENTIFIED ABOUT **300 DIFFERENT STARS** AND THEIR ORBITING PLANETS.

Exploring a Gassy Planet

Trying to walk on _____ is like trying to walk on air—impossible! There's no hard surface,
                        planet

only a swirling mixture of gases that smell like _____ . _____ and I run through them,
                                                    food   friend's name

our final training exercise before _____ another planet in a faraway solar system. In the
                                     verb ending in –ing

haze, we see floating _____ and drops of _____ . A(n) _____ passes by.
                        noun, plural   liquid   noun

I reach out to collect it, and—poof!—it dissolves into a million _____ . We drift along, the
                                                                    noun, plural

gases growing _____ . A(n) _____ covered in _____ floats
                adjective, ending in –er   noun   something sticky

past, and I grab it. It lifts me up and away, until _____ looks like a tiny _____ .
                                                       same friend   noun

I start to feel _____ , so I lick off the _____ and grab a passing _____ .
                  feeling   same sticky something   noun

I nab the next _____ that goes by, and it pulls me downward, back to _____ .
                 noun   same friend

Reunited, we decide to leave—this planet is too _____ !
                                                   adjective

- friend's name
- silly word
- large number
- noun, plural
- verb
- verb ending in –ing
- something scary, plural
- something stinky
- clothing item
- body part
- liquid
- verb
- adverb ending in –ly
- another body part
- noun
- noun
- noun
- adjective
- verb

Fun Fact! ASTRONOMERS CALL AN IDEAL EARTH-LIKE WORLD A "GOLDILOCKS PLANET"— NOT TOO HOT, NOT TOO COLD, BUT JUST RIGHT.

STINK-O-METER

NICE   PU

A New Home?

_____ and I approach planet _____ , _____ light-years away in a distant
<small>friend's name</small>   <small>silly word</small>   <small>large number</small>

solar system. _____ at the International Space Station have sent us here to _____ the
<small>noun, plural</small>   <small>verb</small>

planet for possible colonization. So far, it's not looking good. _____ _____
<small>verb ending in –ing</small>   <small>something scary, plural</small>

that orbit the planet make landing difficult. Immediately after exiting the ship, we notice that the air smells

like _____ . I pull my _____ over my _____ to block
<small>something stinky</small>   <small>clothing item</small>   <small>body part</small>

the odor. We walk to a nearby river of _____ , and I kneel down and _____ it. This is,
<small>liquid</small>   <small>verb</small>

after all, a scientific mission. _____ , I dip in my _____ .
<small>adverb ending in –ly</small>   <small>another body part</small>

Instantly, it turns into a(n) _____ . Freaked out, we run back to the _____ .
<small>noun</small>   <small>noun</small>

There I eat an emergency space _____ that reverses anything alien.
<small>noun</small>

Then I send an official report: "Planet is _____ . Do not _____ here!"
<small>adjective</small>   <small>verb</small>

noun, plural

   number

color

   large number

noun

   adverb ending in –ly

verb ending in –ing

   body part, plural

something pointy

   verb

something slimy

   another body part, plural

loud sound

   verb

silly word

   friend's name

noun, plural

   verb

animal, plural

THE UNIVERSE IS FILLED WITH
VISIBLE LIGHT
AND RADIATION—A KIND OF LIGHT INVISIBLE TO THE NAKED EYE THAT INCLUDES X-RAYS AND RADIO WAVES.

Lights Out!

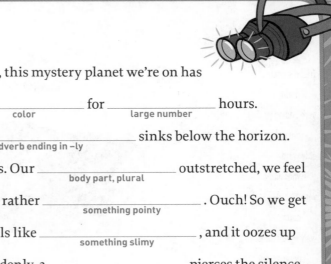

We have to act quickly. According to our _____ (noun, plural) , this mystery planet we're on has

only _____ (number) minutes of daylight. Then it's pitch _____ (color) for _____ (large number) hours.

As we approach a forest, the _____ (noun) _____ (adverb ending in –ly) sinks below the horizon.

Too late—we'll be _____ (verb ending in –ing) in total darkness. Our _____ (body part, plural) outstretched, we feel

our way around. It seems this forest isn't made of leaves but rather _____ (something pointy) . Ouch! So we get

on all fours and _____ (verb) ahead. The ground feels like _____ (something slimy) , and it oozes up

between my _____ (another body part, plural) . Gross! Suddenly, a _____ (loud sound) pierces the silence.

We freeze. Then I feel something _____ (verb) me and I scream, "_____ (silly word) !" But

it's only _____ (friend's name) trying to hand me a pair of night-vision goggles we forgot were in

our _____ (noun, plural) . We put them on and _____ (verb) like _____ (animal, plural) back to the ship.

PEOPLE REPORT THE MOST
UFO SIGHTINGS WHEN
VENUS IS CLOSEST TO EARTH.

- noun, plural
- future year
- friend's name
- number
- verb ending in –ing
- noun
- silly word
- your name
- verb
- noun
- body part, plural
- noun, plural
- food
- animal, plural
- celebrity's name
- noun, plural
- verb
- verb

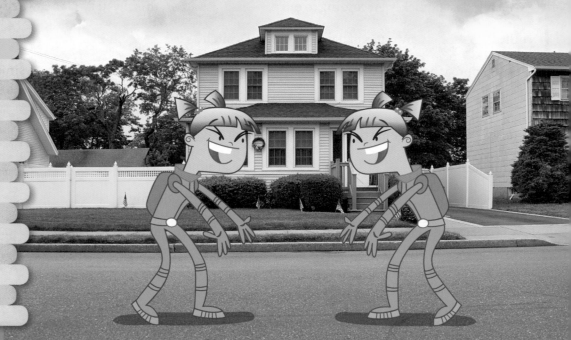

Cosmic Twin

I tap the spaceship's _____ and they flicker to life. The year: _____. The solar
                          noun, plural   future year

system: the same one from which _____ and I received an alien message _____
                                  friend's name   number

months ago. We've arrived here by accident, after _____ into a giant wormhole. We touch
                                                    verb, ending in –ing

down on a glowing _____. There, we get a big surprise: other humans! They greet us by saying,
                    noun

"_____!" before taking us to their leader. I can't believe who it is—me! Or at least someone who
  silly word

looks exactly like me. "I'm _____," (s)he says. "Did you _____ my message?" So that's who
                            your name   verb

sent it—another version of myself living on another _____. We compare our _____
                                                      noun   body part, plural

and _____—they're exactly alike. We talk for hours about our favorite things— _____ ,
      noun, plural   food

_____ , and _____. We finish each other's _____. Eventually, it's
  animal, plural   celebrity's name   noun, plural

time to _____. I _____ my cosmic twin goodbye, and we promise to stay in touch.
          verb   verb

- liquid
  - electronic gadget
- verb ending in –ing
  - noun
- fruit
  - animal
- adjective
  - noun
- adjective
  - something gross
- noun
  - something sticky
- friend's name
  - noun, plural
- something heavy
  - appliance
- clothing item
  - noun, plural
- feeling

Fun Fact! IN 1954, AN EIGHT-POUND (3.6 KG) **METEORITE** CRASHED THROUGH THE ROOF OF AN ALABAMA WOMAN'S HOUSE.

Crash Landing

I've crash-landed before, but this is bad. Our ship is leaking _____ and the _____
liquid electronic gadget

is _____ . Not to mention the _____ is missing; we lost it somewhere over the
verb ending in – ing noun

_____ Nebula. All because we swerved to avoid hitting a(n) _____ but instead hit a
fruit animal

_____ _____ . Now we've got to use what we find here to fix our ship. We split up. I return
adjective noun

with a _____ rock I found in a pile of _____ . It's about the same size
adjective something gross

as the ship's busted _____ , so I rip that out and replace it with the rock, using _____
noun something sticky

to hold it in place. _____ returns with _____ , and we use a(n)
friend's name noun, plural

_____ lying nearby to hammer those into the _____ . Last but
something heavy appliance

not least, we use an old _____ of mine to plug the ship's leak. We climb
clothing item

aboard and fire up the _____ and are _____ when the ship lifts off!
noun, plural feeling

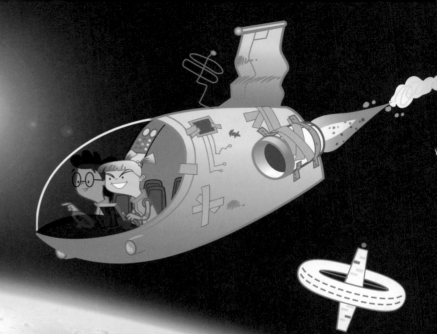

- verb
  - friend's name
- adjective
  - verb
- noun, plural
  - animal, plural
- hometown
  - food
- something gross
  - pet
- silly word
  - adjective
- body part
  - animal sound
- teacher's name
  - same friend's name
- item of clothing, plural
  - noun, plural
- favorite song

 ASTRONAUTS WHO RETURNED TO EARTH FROM EARLY MOON MISSIONS WERE QUARANTINED.

I settle our spaceship into Earth's orbit and finally _____ . We made it!
_____ verb _____

_____ and I have been on a(n) _____ adventure through the cosmos,
friend's name _____ adjective

where I learned how to _____ ; explored _____ ; and met space
_____ verb _____ noun, plural

_____ , aliens, and even another version of myself. It's been awesome, but I'm ready to
animal, plural

return to _____ . I miss _____ that doesn't/don't taste like _____ . And I miss
hometown _____ food _____ something gross

my _____ , who I can't wait to introduce to my alien pet I've brought back from planet _____ .
pet _____ silly word

I reach over and scratch its _____ _____ , and it starts to _____ .
adjective _____ body part _____ animal sound

I think I'll name it _____ . _____ and I debate whether our space
teacher's name _____ same friend's name

_____ that let us see invisible _____ will work on Earth. Then it's time
item of clothing, plural _____ noun, plural

for our final descent. We turn up _____ and enjoy one last ride.
favorite song

Credits

Cover, Edwin Verin/Dreamstime (astronaut), Hanhanpeggy/Dreamstime (satellite), PRIMA/Shutterstock (sun); 4, solarseven/Shutterstock (Background), yavuzunlu/Shutterstock (UPLE); 10, Palto/Shutterstock; 12, wongwean/Shutterstock; 14, mironov/Shutterstock; 16, Guo Yu/Shutterstock; 18, Robert Paul Van Beets/Dreamstime; 20, David Aguilar; 22, NASA; 24, Matej Pavlansky/Shutterstock; 26, Stocktrek/Getty Images; 28, Maria Skaldina/Shutterstock; 30, David Aguilar; 32, Cardens Design/Shutterstock; 34, Luca Oleastri/Dreamstime; 36, Nfsphoto/Dreamstime; 38, wongwean/Shutterstock; 42, rSnapshotPhotos/Shutterstock; 44, Pulok Pattanayak/Dreamstime; 46, G. K./Dreamstime

Published by the National Geographic Society

John M. Fahey, *Chairman of the Board and Chief Executive Officer*
Declan Moore, *Executive Vice President; President, Publishing and Travel*
Melina Gerosa Bellows, *Executive Vice President; Chief Creative Officer, Books, Kids, and Family*

Prepared by the Book Division

Hector Sierra, *Senior Vice President and General Manager*
Nancy Laties Feresten, *Senior Vice President, Kids Publishing and Media*
Jay Sumner, *Director of Photography, Children's Publishing*
Jennifer Emmett, *Vice President, Editorial Director, Children's Books*
Eva Absher-Schantz, *Design Director, Kids Publishing and Media*
R. Gary Colbert, *Production Director*
Jennifer A. Thornton, *Director of Managing Editorial*

Staff for This Book

Kate Olesin, *Project Editor*
James Hiscott, Jr., *Art Director*

Kelley Miller, *Senior Photo Editor*
Ruth Ann Thompson, *Designer*
Ariane Szu-Tu, *Editorial Assistant*
Callie Broaddus, *Design Production Assistant*
Hillary Moloney, *Illustrations Assistant*
Emily Krieger, *Writer*
Dan Sipple, *Illustrator*
Grace Hill and Michael O'Connor, *Associate Managing Editors*
Joan Gossett, *Production Editor*
Lewis R. Bassford, *Production Manager*
Susan Borke, *Legal and Business Affairs*
Kayla Klaben, *Intern*
Angela Modany, *Intern*

Manufacturing and Quality Management

Phillip L. Schlosser, *Senior Vice President*
Chris Brown, *Vice President, NG Book Manufacturing*
George Bounelis, *Vice President, Production Services*
Nicole Elliott, *Manager*
Rachel Faulise, *Manager*
Robert L. Barr, *Manager*

CELEBRATING
◀ **125** ▶
YEARS

The National Geographic Society is one of the world's largest nonprofit scientific and educational organizations. Founded in 1888 to "increase and diffuse geographic knowledge," the Society's mission is to inspire people to care about the planet. It reaches more than 400 million people worldwide each month through its official journal, *National Geographic*, and other magazines; National Geographic Channel; television documentaries; music; radio; films; books; DVDs; maps; exhibitions; live events; school publishing programs; interactive media; and merchandise. National Geographic has funded more than 10,000 scientific research, conservation and exploration projects and supports an education program promoting geographic literacy.

For more information, please call 1-800-NGS LINE (647-5463) or write to the following address:

National Geographic Society, 1145 17th Street N.W., Washington, D.C. 20036-4688 U.S.A.

Visit us online at www.nationalgeographic.com/books

For librarians and teachers: www.ngchildrensbooks.org

More for kids from National Geographic: kids.nationalgeographic.com

For information about special discounts for bulk purchases, please contact National Geographic Books Special Sales: ngspecsales@ngs.org

For rights or permissions inquiries, please contact National Geographic Books Subsidiary Rights: ngbookrights@ngs.org

ISBN: 978-1-4263-1354-7

Printed in Hong Kong

13/THK/1